FROM

TRIALS

TO

TESTIMONY

When the Test Becomes the Story

That Sets Others Free

DR. DERRICK WASHINGTON

"Praise be to the God and Father of our Lord Jesus Christ, the Father of compassion and the God of all comfort,
who comforts us in all our troubles, so that we can comfort those in any trouble with the comfort we ourselves receive from God."

—2 Corinthians 1:3-4

Cover design and internal layout by Inspiring Faith By DW

ISBN: 979-8-218-72507-5 (paperback)

Printed in the United States of America

First Edition

For more information, visit: www.inspiringfaithbydw.com

Dedication

To my incredible wife Sharon—your unwavering love, prayers, and strength have carried me through some of the darkest seasons. Thank you for being my partner, my peace, and my encouragement.

To my mother Louise—your faith and resilience have shaped who I am. You've shown me what it means to persevere with grace and trust God through it all.

To my children (Akeem, DaJiah, Jerrion, Kaleb)—you are my legacy. May you always know the power of faith, family, and never giving up.

To my brother Lesel, grandkids (Prince and J'La), my family, and my faithful friends—thank you for standing beside me, praying for me, and believing in me when I couldn't see the way forward.

To my father Les, grandmother Vera, grandparents Eva & OC, and loved ones who have gone to be with the Lord—your memory lives on in every page. I carry your strength, your wisdom, and your love with me.

And to every person who has ever been broken but not defeated... who has cried in silence yet continued to believe... who turned their pain into praise—**this book is for you.** May you find healing, hope, and freedom in your own testimony. May you be reminded that even in your darkest hour, God is still writing your story.

Preface

I never imagined that the most painful chapters of my life would one day become the very pages others would read for hope. This book was birthed in the middle of breakdowns, battles, and breathless moments. It was not written from a mountaintop, but from a valley—a place of wrestling, weeping, and wondering if I would ever rise again.

From Trials to Testimony is not just a book. It's a mirror. It reflects the journey of a soul who's walked through fire and found faith, who's been broken and discovered purpose, who's gasped for breath and still found something to say. Every chapter was penned through prayer, through tears, through moments of silence when only God could hear the cries I didn't have the strength to speak.

If you've ever felt like life knocked the wind out of you, if you've ever stood at the edge of giving up, if you've ever wondered whether your pain has a point—this book is for you. You are not alone. And your story is not over.

Each page is a piece of my journey, but I believe God will use it to speak into yours. I didn't write this to impress you—I wrote it to walk with you. To remind you that grace is real, healing is possible, and your testimony is being written even now.

Thank you for allowing me to share my heart. May these words remind you that God does His best work in the mess, and that every trial can become the soil of your testimony.

With grace and gratitude,
Dr. Derrick Washington

Abstract

From Trials to Testimony is a deeply personal and spiritually rich account of how God transforms our darkest moments into divine messages of hope. Drawing from decades of personal affliction, loss, healing, and redemption, Dr. Derrick Washington shares ten pivotal chapters of his life journey, each filled with scriptural insight, heartfelt reflection, and triumphant faith. This book invites readers to confront their own pain, discover purpose in hardship, and embrace the testimony God is writing through their trials. With prayers and guided reflection throughout, this work is both a companion for personal healing and a powerful tool for ministry, small groups, and teaching.

Table of Content

Introduction

Everyone has a story—but not every story is told. Some of the most powerful testimonies are birthed in silence, shaped by suffering, and strengthened in seasons where it felt like no one was listening. This book is my story—but it's also yours. It's for anyone who has faced moments so dark that the light felt out of reach. For anyone who has cried in secret, wrestled with questions, and clung to faith by a thread. It's for those who are still standing, not because they never fell, but because grace caught them when they did.

From Trials to Testimony was born out of pain—but redeemed by purpose. Through sickness, surgeries, loss, grief, and unexpected valleys, I've come to see that the very tests we try to hide are the ones God wants to use to set others free. This book doesn't sugarcoat the suffering. Instead, it leans into it, unwraps the layers, and uncovers the glory of God working behind the scenes.

As you turn these pages, you'll find not just chapters, but checkpoints—sacred places where God met me in my weakness and showed Himself strong. My prayer is that each testimony inspires you to reflect, to heal, and most of all, to hope. You don't have to have all the answers. You don't even have to feel strong. You just need to know that you're not alone—and that your story matters.

This is not just a book. It's an altar. It's a mirror. It's a call to see your pain through the eyes of promise. And it's an invitation—

to trust that your test might just be the key to someone else's breakthrough. So, whether you're in the fire or on the other side of it, may these words remind you: you're still here for a reason. And God is not done writing your testimony.

With hope and healing,
Dr. Derrick Washington

Chapter 1

The Breaking Point

Psalm 34:18

"The Lord is close to the brokenhearted and saves those who are crushed in spirit."

Introduction

Life has a way of hitting us without warning. At some point, life brings each of us to our knees—a sudden loss, a deep betrayal, or an overwhelming crisis. For me, that moment was the unexpected death of my father on December 18, 1999. Grief tore into my world, shaking my faith and challenging everything I believed. This was my breaking point. But what I didn't know at the time was that it was also the beginning of a deeper journey with God. It was in this breaking point where God's rebuilding began. This chapter invites you to reflect on the places where you've felt shattered as we explore what happens when tragedy pushes us to our breaking point and discover how God meets us precisely there.

Key Takeaway:

"Your lowest moment can become the beginning of your greatest transformation."

Expanded Reflection

I had always believed God was a protector, but as I stood over my father's hospital bed, questions flooded my mind. Where was God in this? Why now? Why him? My theology clashed with my reality. And in that moment, I realized faith doesn't always mean answers—it means holding on when you have none.

Father's unexpected death (1999–2000)

Have you ever felt like everything you once trusted was slipping through your fingers? I remember a season in my life when the weight of loss and disappointment pressed so heavily on my heart that I wondered if I would ever find peace again.

The pain was compounded by a series of family losses.

My mother's father died in 1996, my mother's mother passed away in 1997, and then my own father in 1999. It felt like my world had shattered into pieces, and I couldn't see how God was working in the midst of the pain.

This breaking point felt like the end of hope, but it became the beginning of a powerful transformation. To understand this transformation, let me take you back.

In 1991, I joined the Navy at the early age of 17. My first duty station after bootcamp was in Goose Creek, South Carolina.

I spent four and a half years there before transferring to the Navy Submarine Base Kings Bay in St. Mary's, Georgia in 1996. It was here, at the end of my tour in 1999, that my breaking point would unfold.

December had arrived—the holidays were near. I had just been granted leave to go home for Christmas. My leave period started on that Thursday December 16th. My brother and I decided to surprise our family in Monroe, Louisiana. Our plan was to show up unannounced on Monday, December 20th. But for safety, I called my father, Les Washington, to let him know our plans.

To my surprise, he told me he wouldn't be there as he stated, "By the time y'all get here you guys would have missed me." He was scheduled for a minor outpatient procedure on December 17th at

Barksdale Air Force Base Medical Hospital and then planned to travel to Los Angeles on the 19th to visit his brothers.

Who would have thought that this conversation would become the last time I would ever speak to my father.

Determined to see him before he left, my brother and I left earlier—on Friday, December 17th—and arrived early the next morning.

Thinking we had successfully pulled off our surprise, I called my dad's house.

No answer.

I tried my mom.

Still no answer.

Confused, I called a cousin, hoping for clarity.

Sadly, what came next threw us into a frantic notion as we were met with the worst news that no one would ever want to hear.

His words sent shockwaves through my soul: "He's gone.

Your Daddy's gone."

Now, to anyone's imagination, it's not hard to see how this kind of confused me because he was presenting it as in a code of secrecy as he did not want to give me any details which made things that much worse as my anxiety shot to the roof.

I'm stressing not understanding the meaning, as my heart began racing and my brother panicking.

Stunned, confused, and in a panic, we rushed to my mother's house.

As we pulled into the driveway, my mother rushed out with tears in her eyes and hugged me and my brother so tightly which really made our hearts pound even harder with confusion, sorrow, and despair.

I asked her what was going on and what happened, and the next words that came out of her mouth shattered my whole world.

She said words I will never forget: "Your Daddy's gone.

He is brain dead." My knees buckled.

My heart sank.

Tears streamed uncontrollably down my face.

She told us he was on life support, and we would be heading to Shreveport the next morning to meet with the doctors.

Then, that next morning we headed to Shreveport. When we arrived nothing could have prepared me for what I saw at the hospital.

Tubes ran across his body.

The rhythmic sound of the breathing machine echoed in the room on every inhale and exhale.

The way his body lay there lifeless.

I could not believe it; my hero lay there motionless.

I couldn't speak.

I couldn't breathe.

I couldn't move and was afraid to even touch him.

The pain consumed me in a way that all I saw was him and that machine.

The doctor enters the room and presents us with the details.

He explained that my father had suffered three heart attacks and was in a vegetative state with little to no brain activity.

He gave us a grim 10% chance of survival.

Even if he lived, he would never regain full functionality.

The doctor then asked us if we wanted to remove life support or authorize resuscitation should another heart attack occur.

From that very moment I totally lost every foundational principle I knew, especially praying.

My eyes full of tears dried up and turned to anger as I took those comments as a sign of total disrespect and disregard for my father and us.

At that moment, everything was clear again as I immediately responded for all of us as I emphatically stated, "A 10% chance is still a chance. Do not take him off the machine and revive him if needed."

Later that day, after returning to Monroe (some 99 miles away), we received the call—my father had suffered another heart attack, and they could not revive him.

It felt like he had waited just long enough for us to say goodbye.

The thought of him suffering during our drive back to Monroe haunted me.

In the days that followed, I couldn't pray. I couldn't eat. I shut down emotionally and stuffed everything inside.

After the funeral, I had to hold myself together for my mother and brother. The grief never fully left. I reported to my new duty station in Norfolk, Virginia, carrying my pain, my anger, my confusion, and emotional exhaustion. What should have been an exciting move felt unbearable.

But God wasn't finished. At my new duty station, He sent me a messenger—a colleague we will call George, a Reverend of the Word of God. George was assigned to my department in Operations. Looking back, I now see how God was working. Even in silence, He was orchestrating comfort.

George became a blessing in disguise.

He reeled me back in.

He poured into me daily with prayer, Scripture, and encouragement.

He would often say, "God has something special for you to do.

He has called you, even in the midst of your pain." Slowly, I began to feel again.

I began to believe again.

Through George, God reminded me that I was never alone.

Influence

At my new duty station, I met George—a colleague and minister.

He didn't lecture or force answers.

He simply showed up.

Sometimes it was a prayer, a Scripture note, or just silent presence.

Through George, I slowly rediscovered my faith.

God hadn't left me.

He was working through the people around me.

Scripture Insight

Psalm 34:18 and 2 Corinthians 1:3-4 became anchors during that season:

Psalm 34:18 became my anchor: "The Lord is close to the brokenhearted and saves those who are crushed in spirit." David, the psalmist, knew deep pain.

He understood deep suffering.

He knew what it meant to face trials that could have crushed his spirit, yet he clung to God's presence because he also knew God's nearness.

Like David, I found comfort in knowing that our breaking points are not the end. They are not where God abandons us —they are where God's saving power becomes most evident.

This verse is a beautiful reminder that God does not turn away from our pain; rather, He draws near when we are hurting the most.

Another verse that deeply resonated with me during that season is 2 Corinthians 1:3–4 (NIV): "Praise be to the God and Father of our Lord Jesus Christ, the Father of compassion and the God of all comfort, who comforts us in all our troubles, so that we can comfort those in any trouble with the comfort we ourselves receive from God."

This verse showed me that my pain wasn't pointless.

God didn't just comfort me to make me feel better—He comforted me to equip me.

George wasn't just a friend; he was a vessel of God's comfort, preparing me to one day do the same for others.

The comfort we receive becomes the comfort we give, and that is how testimony is born out of trial.

God's compassion, and his presence helped me walk back into the arms of grace.

George's care showed me that comfort is meant to be passed on. In that moment, I realized that what I had received would one day be someone else's breakthrough.

Biblical Pattern of Breaking Points

Scripture is filled with people whose pain became purpose. Job, Joseph, and David all faced seasons where their faith was tested. Yet through it all, God proved faithful. Our breaking doesn't disqualify us—it prepares us for more.

"In the silence of sorrow, He whispered peace. In the weight of grief, He carried me. In the absence of answers, He became my anchor."

Reflection Questions

1. What was a "breaking point" moment in your life?
2. How did that moment impact your view of God or yourself?
3. What step can you take today to trust God more deeply through this?

Application

Even when life breaks you, God's presence holds you together. Recognize that pain is not the end but often the doorway to God's deeper presence.

- Take time to journal or pray about your own "breaking point."
- Instead of asking "Why me?" begin to ask, "What now, Lord?" and "What are You showing me through this?"

Prayer & Encouragement

Prayer:

God, we bring You the broken pieces of our lives. In moments when we feel shattered and weak, remind us that You are near.

We don't always understand why things happened the way they did, but we trust You to bring beauty from our brokenness. Heal the parts of us that still ache. Remind us that even in our breaking, You are building something new.

Remind us that we are never too far for You to reach, rescue, and restore. Thank You for turning our trials into testimony and for using our brokenness to bring glory to Your name.

Strengthen us to move forward in faith and hope. Amen.

Encouragement

If you're at your breaking point, know this: God is not distant from your pain. He is **closest** when life feels most fragile. What shattered your heart didn't surprise God—it became His invitation to begin a deeper work in you.

You may not feel strong, but you don't have to be.

God's strength shows up **right where you are weak**.

The tears you cry in private are seen by the One who collects every single one.

And just like He sent George to walk with me in my valley, **He will send what you need when you need it**.

Your brokenness is not the end—it's the birthplace of something sacred. This season may feel like loss, but it may actually be **laying the foundation** for your healing, your calling, and your testimony. One day, your story will bring someone else back to life.

So, breathe. Cry. Pray. But don't give up. God is with you in the breaking. And He's already preparing your rebuilding.

Quote to Remember:
"God doesn't waste brokenness—He builds with it."

Journal / Notes:

(Write your reflections here)

Chapter 2

When God Feels Silent

Psalm 13:1
"How long, Lord? Will you forget me forever? How long will you hide your face from me?"

Romans 8:18
"I consider that our present sufferings are not worth comparing with the glory that will be revealed in us."

Introduction

Silence from heaven doesn't mean absence. There are seasons when we pray and wait...and wait... and wait.

It feels like heaven has gone quiet. But even when God seems silent, He is still present and still working.

This chapter will help you process what it means to trust God in the silence and what that silence can produce in your soul.

It invites you to see your storm through a lens of hope, finding purpose in the midst of pain.

Key Takeaway:

"Faith grows strongest in the silence when God seems far away."

Expanded Reflection

The silence of God is not the absence of God. There are moments when heaven feels closed, when every prayer feels like it's bouncing off the ceiling.

Yet, this silence can become sacred. It can deepen faith, refine character, and force us to confront what we really believe.

Silence has a way of exposing the noise inside us—the fears, doubts, and insecurities. But it also creates space for trust to grow. When answers don't come and healing delays, we learn to rest in God's character rather than His visible hand.

14

Struggling with employment despite doctorate (2023)
Habakkuk 2:3
"Though it lingers, wait for it; it will certainly come and will not delay."

Initial disability challenges (2009)
Romans 8:25
"But if we hope for what we do not yet have, we wait for it patiently."

There are seasons when God's presence feels distant—when our prayers seem to echo back without response, and silence becomes the loudest sound in our hearts.

I've walked through those quiet valleys, questioning if God had forgotten me.

But in that silence, I discovered something deeper: a trust that only grows in the absence of answers, and a patience that isn't born in comfort, but in the furnace of waiting.

In 2023, after earning my doctorate, I found myself unemployed.

I had reached what should have been a milestone—years of academic sacrifice, long nights, perseverance through health struggles—and yet, it felt like I was standing at a locked door. Opportunities weren't opening.

I cried out, "God, where are You?" I had expected celebration, but what followed was silence.

It wasn't just a professional disappointment, it was personal.

It felt like my worth was being questioned by the very silence of heaven.

Imagine reaching the summit of your profession only to feel like you're stuck on the ground floor, peering in through the window.

Job fair after job fair.

Application after application.

And still—dead silence.

Not even a whisper.

What I learned a long time ago is to trust God no matter what.

Proverbs 3:5–6 became my rallying cry in moments such as these.

My motto reminded me: "Trust in the Lord with all your heart, and lean not on your own understanding; in all your ways acknowledge Him, and He shall direct your paths." This keeps me grounded, refusing to let the enemy plant negative thoughts in my mind.

But this wasn't my first waiting season.

In 2009, I began navigating life with a disability.

Chronic illness showed up like an uninvited guest and never left.

Some days I couldn't get out of bed.

Some nights, sleep evaded me as pain consumed my body.

I lost count of the medical appointments, the treatments, the slow progress. I wasn't just physically weak—I was spiritually weary. Yet even then, in the stillness and stagnation, God was present.

Time after time, when rheumatoid arthritis and fibromyalgia flares occur, it can feel like your body is betraying you.

Frustration sets in.

You want to pray—but your lips tremble with questions instead of praises.

You expect a sigh of relief or a word of comfort to come from God.

And when the reply doesn't come, or not when you expect it, you start to wonder: Is God hearing my prayers? Has He turned His back on me? Am I being punished, or is there something deeper He's trying to teach me through this suffering?

Living with these conditions means constantly being misunderstood.

Because it's invisible, people assume you're fine.

But not all battles are visible.

Some of the hardest fights are waged behind closed doors—where faith whispers what flesh wants to scream.

On the outside, I smiled.

But on the inside, my body and soul cried out for relief.

That silence became a crucible where a deeper faith was forged—not loud, but enduring.

Not flashy, but rooted.

God, who sees all and knows all, became the only One who truly understood what I was carrying.

Habakkuk 2:3 spoke directly to my soul:
"Though it lingers, wait for it; it will certainly come and will not delay."

Romans 8:25 echoed it:
"But if we hope for what we do not yet have, we wait for it patiently."

During those quiet seasons, journaling became a lifeline. I began writing down my prayers, even when I felt God wasn't answering. Looking back, I see how those entries traced my journey from despair to renewed trust.

These verses didn't just comfort me—they taught me how to breathe when hope felt delayed. They reminded me that silence is not absence. It is often God's way of preparing us for what we're not yet ready to carry.

Looking back, I can now say: God's silence was never abandonment.

It was strategy.

It was strength-building.

It was sacred.

And though I'm still learning to fully trust when heaven is quiet, I can say with assurance—He was there all along.

Maybe not in the way I asked, but always in the way I needed.

Influence

The silent seasons birthed empathy in me. They taught me to recognize the pain in others' eyes, to listen deeper, and to minister from a place of understanding. My story became a mirror for others walking through long nights with no visible dawn.

Silence trains you to become a comforter—not with empty words, but with presence, prayer, and compassion.

One Sunday after service, I noticed a young man lingering quietly in the back row, shoulders slumped, eyes heavy with a weight he hadn't spoken.

I didn't approach with advice or a sermon—I simply sat beside him.

After a few minutes of silence, he opened up.

He shared how he was battling a chronic condition that no one around him seemed to understand, and how the pressure to appear strong was slowly breaking him down.

I offered a glimpse into my own journey—not to compare pain, but to let him know he wasn't alone in his.

That day, I didn't offer solutions.

What I gave was presence—and in that sacred stillness, peace began to settle in his heart.

Sometimes ministry isn't in the words we speak, but in the willingness to be present, especially when someone feels invisible in their fire.

Scripture Insight

Psalm 13:1 — "How long, Lord? Will you forget me forever? How long will you hide your face from me?"

"How long, Lord?" I had asked that same question so many times. But just like David, I found strength in being honest with God. His shoulders are big enough for our questions.

Romans 8:18 — "I consider that our present sufferings are not worth comparing with the glory that will be revealed in us."

"Our present sufferings…" That verse gave me hope that what I was going through wouldn't be wasted—that God was still writing.

Biblical Pattern or Breaking Points
Scripture is filled with people who endured God's silence before their breakthrough.

Hannah wept in silence for years before Samuel was born. Her anguish was real, but so was her breakthrough. God often hides His greatest miracles in seasons of delayed answers.

Job experienced the silence of God as he lost everything, but even in silence, God was sovereign and restored him.

Jesus, in Gethsemane, asked for the cup to pass—but He found no escape, only endurance. The silence of the Father didn't stop the redemption of the world.

Habakkuk waited for an answer—and was told to *write the vision and wait for it*.

The silence is not punishment—it's preparation. God is building something beneath the surface that cannot yet be seen.

Reflection Questions

1. Have you ever felt abandoned by God? What led to that feeling?
2. What did silence from God teach you about trust or patience?
3. How do you keep your faith alive during silent seasons?
4. What can you do to remain spiritually strong even when answers don't come?

Application

Your silent battle is not unseen—God is strengthening your faith through it. Use silence as an invitation, not an insult. During seasons when God feels distant:

- Establish spiritual disciplines (fasting, meditative prayer, or Scripture memory) that keep you anchored.

- Keep a journal of prayers—so when God does answer, you remember His faithfulness.
- Trust that growth is happening underground before fruit is visible.

Prayer & Encouragement

Prayer:

Lord, help us trust even when we cannot hear Your voice. Teach us to wait patiently for Your timing and believe that Your silence doesn't mean You've stopped working. Lord, You see what others don't. You hear our bodies and souls when they groan with pain. Give us the strength to keep walking, the faith to keep trusting, and the grace to believe You're not done with us yet.

We surrender our questions, our timelines, and our fears into Your hands. You are the God who sees, even when we don't see the way forward. Be near to us in the silence. Amen.

Encouragement

Maybe you're reading this and the silence still surrounds you. I don't have all the answers, but I do know this: your silence is not wasted. It's the soil where deeper faith grows. Keep holding on. The story isn't over.

If you're in a season of silence, don't confuse it with abandonment. God's silence is not His absence—it's His invitation to trust Him in the dark. What feels like a "no" or "not yet" might be God's way of deepening your roots so your faith can stand firm in the storm. Your cries are heard, your tears are seen, and your waiting is not in vain. Silence doesn't mean God has stopped speaking—it may mean He's preparing something you're not ready to see just yet.

Hold on. Keep praying.

Keep trusting.

God is closer than you feel and more faithful than you know.

Quote to Remember:
"Heaven may be silent, but God is still speaking through your survival."

Journal / Notes:

(Write your reflections here)

Chapter 3

When the Bottom Falls Out

Degenerative spinal disease and surgeries
Deuteronomy 8:2 — "Remember how the Lord your God led
you through the wilderness...to humble and test you."

Ordination amidst challenges (2016)
2 Corinthians 4:8-9 — "We are hard pressed on every side, but
not crushed; perplexed, but not in despair; persecuted, but not
abandoned; struck down, but not destroyed."

James 1:12 – "Blessed is the one who perseveres under trial..."

Introduction

The wilderness isn't just a place of wandering—it's a place of preparation. God often leads us into seasons of isolation, hardship, and waiting to teach us who He is and who we are. These dry, silent seasons are not signs of abandonment but invitations to grow, surrender, and be refined. In this chapter, we'll explore what happens when the bottom falls out—and how that collapse often becomes the foundation for something new.

Key Takeaway:

"God's refining comes in the wilderness seasons of life. What feels like falling apart may be God pulling you together."

Expanded Reflection

The wilderness is not just a barren place—it's a sacred space where God refines, humbles, and draws us close.

It strips away our comforts, disrupts our expectations, and forces us to confront the core of our faith.

In those dry and weary places, God reveals that His presence does not depend on our circumstances.

Deuteronomy 8:2 tells us that God led the Israelites through the wilderness to humble and test them.

That journey wasn't random—it was intentional.

It was about shaping their hearts, revealing their dependence, and preparing them for promise.

In the same way, our wilderness seasons aren't wasted.

They reveal what's in us, burn away what doesn't belong, and make room for God's sustaining grace.

When life collapses—when health deteriorates, when dreams fall apart, when the ground beneath us gives way—we discover that God is the only firm foundation. The bottom falling out isn't the end; it's often the beginning of something deeper. That's where grace meets us.

2 Corinthians 4:8–9 reminds us: "We are hard pressed on every side, but not crushed; perplexed, but not in despair..." These verses give language to the tension we often feel—pushed but still standing, broken but not destroyed.

It is in this tension where perseverance is born, where the Spirit of God does His quiet, redeeming work.

God's refining often comes disguised as hardship.

His rebuilding often starts at the site of our greatest collapse.

He isn't waiting on the other side of your trial—He's right there in the middle of it, reshaping you for the life ahead.

Even in the most unexpected collapse, God is still crafting a future.

He doesn't need everything to go right in order to write a good ending.

Sometimes the breaking point becomes the birthplace of our deepest testimony.

Story/Testimony

There's something deeply disorienting about watching your carefully constructed life unravel one piece at a time.

I thought I had it all figured out—career plans, personal goals, and a future I could clearly envision.

But one diagnosis shifted everything.

Degenerative spinal disease became the unwanted intruder in my story, rewriting my daily reality with pain, limitations, and the loss of independence.

Suddenly, I found myself unable to do the most basic tasks without pain.

I went from active and driven to constantly fatigued, dependent, and uncertain.

I wasn't just dealing with physical symptoms—I was grappling with the emotional toll of watching my life change before my eyes.

I was navigating disability paperwork, stacks of unpaid bills, and a growing sense of despair.

My faith, once so strong, began to tremble under the weight of unanswered questions.

I feared I was losing more than my health—I feared I was losing myself.

But it was at that breaking point—when I had nothing left to hold onto—that I discovered God was already there, waiting. He wasn't distant. He wasn't angry. He was near. The wilderness wasn't evidence of His absence; it was the classroom of His presence.

The pain didn't vanish. The surgeries didn't erase the struggle. But something deeper was happening inside me. I began to understand that this wilderness was not the end of my story. It was where God was doing some of His most important work—humbling me, strengthening me, and reshaping my heart.

In 2016, amid this season of pain and uncertainty, I was ordained into ministry.That may seem like a contradiction—being commissioned while feeling broken.

But God often calls us in the middle of the storm, not after it has passed.

That moment of ordination became a beacon of hope.

It reminded me that even when everything else was falling apart, God's calling was still intact.

Influence

The wilderness stripped away what I thought I needed and taught me to rely on what I truly needed—God's presence. It exposed my fragility and revealed His faithfulness. I began to view suffering differently. It wasn't just something to endure but something God could use.

I became more compassionate. I recognized the silent pain behind people's smiles. I learned to sit with others in their brokenness without rushing to fix them. Because I knew what it meant to be crushed but not destroyed, I could better serve others walking through similar valleys.

Scripture Insight

In Deuteronomy 8:2, Moses reminds the Israelites, "Remember how the Lord your God led you all the way in the wilderness these forty years, to humble and test you in order to know what was in your heart..." The wilderness was a testing ground that shaped their character and faith. Our wilderness seasons are similar — times God uses to refine and prepare us for His promises.

Just like the Israelites, we are led through dry seasons to reveal the condition of our hearts—and to shape our dependence on God.

2 Corinthians 4:8–9 is a powerful reminder that pressure doesn't have to crush us. We may feel broken, but we are never forsaken. Paul's words show us that the fire tests us, but God sustains us.

James 1:12 affirms that endurance is not just survival—it's a blessing. There's a crown for those who persevere.

When life falls apart, God doesn't. He is a steady presence in the storm, often doing His deepest work when our foundations are shaking. What feels like the end may actually be the beginning of transformation.

Biblical Pattern of Breaking Points

God often meets His people in the wilderness:

- **Moses** met God at a burning bush in exile.
- **Elijah** heard God's whisper in a cave after running in fear.
- **Jesus** faced temptation in the wilderness before beginning His ministry.

Breaking points are not endings. They are holy thresholds.

Reflection Questions

1. What "wilderness" seasons have you experienced?
2. What lessons or growth came out of those difficult times?
3. How did God use isolation or stillness to draw you closer?

Application

There are moments in life when it feels like the ground beneath you disappears—job loss, diagnosis, betrayal, heartbreak. These are the times when we ask, "Where is God?" The answer: He's right there, catching you.

Try these steps:

- **Storm Journal**: Begin a daily "storm journal" where you write how God is sustaining you even when nothing around you changes.
- **Worship Weapon**: Create a worship playlist with songs that speak to God's faithfulness. Let praise be your weapon during breakdowns.
- **Speak the Word**: Memorize *Isaiah 41:10* or *Psalm 46:1–2* and declare them daily, especially when anxiety or fear tries to return.

Prayer & Encouragement

Prayer:

Jesus, when the bottom falls out, be the foundation we land on. In the midst of confusion and pain, remind us that we are not abandoned.

Let our broken pieces fall into Your hands. Shape them into a testimony. Help us trust that You are using this wilderness to prepare us, not punish us. Be our strength when we have none. Amen.

Encouragement

You may feel like life is unraveling, but God is weaving something new. You are not forgotten. You are being formed. Don't fear the fall—grace will catch you every time.

Quote to Remember:
"When life collapses, grace becomes the ground you stand on."

Journal / Notes:

(Write your reflections here)

Chapter 4

Faith In the Fire

TIA (Transient Ischemic Attack (2011)
Isaiah 43:2

*"When you pass through the waters, I will be with you; and when you pass through the rivers, they will not sweep over you. **When you walk through the fire, you will not be burned;** the flames will not set you ablaze."*

2 Corinthians 12:9

"My grace is sufficient for you, for my power is made perfect in weakness."

Isaiah 43:19

"See, I am doing a new thing! Now it springs up; do you not perceive it?"

Jeremiah 1:5

"Before I formed you in the womb I knew you, before you were born I set you apart..."

Introduction

Sometimes life feels like a furnace. Circumstances get hotter, and faith is refined through the flames. But God never abandons you in the fire—He steps in with you. This chapter is about recognizing when God is doing something new and stepping into it with faith. Join me as we uncover how your trials today can become tomorrow's testimonies.

Key Takeaway:

"Hope rises when we least expect it and shifts our story forever. God's grace sustains us when we have nothing left to give. The fire doesn't mean God has left you. It means He's preparing something in you that only pressure can produce."

Expanded Reflection

Faith is easy when life is predictable. But when everything feels like it's falling apart—when you're under physical, emotional, or spiritual pressure—that's when real faith is tested.

The "fire" can be a hospital room, a phone call with devastating news, a betrayal, a breakdown, or a battle with your own body.

It strips away the illusion of control. It silences the noise of comfort. And it forces you to answer one question:
Do I still trust God when nothing makes sense?

God doesn't always offer instant explanations. Sometimes He lets the fire purify more than it burns. He uses the unknown to develop trust. He allows the heat to expose what we really believe.

But Isaiah 43 doesn't say *"if"* you walk through the fire—it says *"when."* Which means fire is inevitable... but **so is God's presence in it**.
The fire doesn't get the final say. **God does.**

The fire is not just a test—it's a place of transformation. I've learned that God doesn't always remove the flames, but He changes us within them. Sometimes the greatest evidence of God's presence isn't in the miracle that delivers you, but in the strength that sustains you through it.

The fire reveals what's real. It strips away the surface and exposes the core of your faith. Faith isn't proven on the mountaintop—it's forged in the furnace.

Story/Testimony

I remember the fear in my chest more than the pain.

It started like a flicker—a strange tightness in my chest, a racing heartbeat, and an overwhelming sense that something wasn't right.

In 2011, I was rushed to the emergency room by ambulance.

What I thought was maybe just fatigue or stress turned out to be far more serious.

The doctors said I had experienced a Transient Ischemic Attack (TIA)—a warning stroke.

And while that diagnosis alone was terrifying, the real fire was just beginning.

Tests revealed I had severely low potassium levels, which caused irregular heart rhythms and strong palpitations.

But even with that clue, there was no clear answer—no confirmed reason why my potassium had dropped so dangerously.

I was admitted for what became a full seven-day hospital stay filled with blood tests, monitors, questions, and silence.

Each day passed slowly. I was hooked up to wires and machines, surrounded by professionals, but still living with uncertainty. I kept waiting for a breakthrough. A diagnosis. A "here's what's wrong, and here's how we'll fix it." But that clarity never came.

I wasn't just fighting a physical battle. I was facing a spiritual crisis.

How could I trust God when I didn't know what was happening inside my own body?

How could I have faith when I was surrounded by unanswered questions?

There's something deeply humbling about being helpless. Being in a hospital bed while doctors shrug, tests contradict each other, and answers stay just out of reach feels like fire. It burns away your assumptions. It melts your confidence.

But here's what I learned: faith isn't forged on the mountaintop—it's refined in the fire.

In that hospital room, with monitors beeping and fear whispering every hour, I met God in a different way. Not as a quick fixer, but as a faithful presence. Not in the healing, but in the holding.

I walked out of that hospital still uncertain. Still physically weak. Still without a full diagnosis. But I walked out differently. More grounded. More grateful. More aware of grace.

The physical struggle was real, but the spiritual fire burned deeper.

I had to trust that God wasn't done with me yet.

That the same God who called me before birth (Jeremiah 1:5) would carry me through the valley of death.

That fire became a refining moment, not a destroying one.

Influence

What we survive becomes someone else's survival guide. When people see you endure hardship with faith, it reminds them that endurance is possible.

Even in seasons of pain, people are watching how you walk. Your steady steps—even when uncertain—preach louder than any sermon. My endurance through sickness, loss, and confusion became a silent ministry that encouraged others to keep trusting, even when they couldn't trace God.

Scripture Insight

Our faith is often tested not in comfort but under the intense heat of life's hardest trials. Experiencing family losses back-to-back over recent years has stretched and tested my faith in unimaginable ways.

One key takeaway is that faith not only survives the fire but emerges stronger, refined, and ready to testify to the goodness of God.

- **Isaiah 43:2** promises us we will pass *through* the fire—not be consumed by it.
- **2 Corinthians 12:9** reminds us that His strength is made perfect in our weakness.

- **Isaiah 43:19** shows that even in the fire, God is doing a new thing—sometimes the fire clears space for the new to spring up.

Biblical Pattern of Breaking Points

- **Shadrach, Meshach, and Abednego** weren't spared from the fire—but the presence of the *Fourth Man* in the furnace made all the difference (Daniel 3).
- "Like **Shadrach, Meshach, and Abednego**, I've learned that God's presence is sometimes clearest in the hottest seasons…"
- **Job's losses** refined his understanding of God and multiplied his blessings (Job 42).
- **Paul**, despite his thorn, declared that God's grace was sufficient for every weakness.

In each case, fire didn't end the story—it revealed God's hand and deepened their testimony.

Reflection Questions

1. What personal "fires" have you walked through, and how did they test your faith?
2. In what ways has God refined you through hardship rather than removing it?
3. Can you look back and identify the "Fourth Man" moments—where God showed up in unexpected ways?
4. What is God doing *new* in your life even while the fire still burns?

Application

- Journal about one season in your life where the fire refined you.
- Write down the "fruit" or lessons you've carried out of the flames.
- Declare this truth aloud daily: *"God is with me in the fire, and I will not be consumed."*

Prayer & Encouragement

Prayer:

*Father, thank You for not abandoning us in the fire. You didn't promise to keep **us** from trials, but You promised to be with us through them.*

*Refine us, not just to remove the pain—but to reveal **Your purpose** in our lives. Strengthen our **faith** where it feels weak. Let **our story** shine with **Your glory**, even when the smoke still lingers.*

*Turn **our fire** into fuel—fuel to worship, to witness, and to walk in victory. Amen.*

Encouragement

You're not just walking through fire—you're being *forged* in it. What feels like destruction is really preparation. God is burning away what no longer serves you and awakening something new within you.

You're coming out of this—stronger, purer, and clearer. Your faith may feel fragile, but it's fire-tested. And what God refines, He never wastes. Stand strong. Even the fire has a purpose.

Quote to Remember:
"The fire you fear may be the furnace where your faith is forged."

Journal / Notes:
(Write your reflections here)

Chapter 5

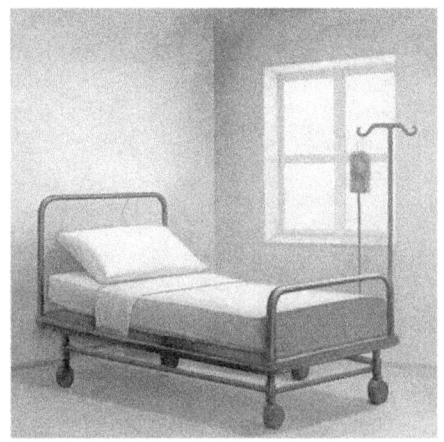

Recovery Room

Cervical surgery and recovery (2018)
Isaiah 40:31
"...those who hope in the Lord will renew their strength."

Jeremiah 30:17
"But I will restore you to health and heal your wounds,'
declares the Lord."

Vocal cord implant and restored voice
Psalm 30:11-12

"You turned my wailing into dancing; you removed my sackcloth and clothed me with joy..."

Introduction

Every testimony has a turning point—a moment where the darkness begins to lift, and the light starts to shine through. Sometimes it's gradual, and other times, it's a breakthrough. When we reach the end of ourselves, God steps in. His grace doesn't just cover our sins—it sustains us in weakness. This chapter reminds you that you were never meant to carry the weight alone. Grace carries what you cannot.

Key Takeaway:

"Healing isn't instant, but God is present in every step of recovery."

Expanded Reflection

Recovery isn't just physical—it's emotional, mental, and spiritual. After surgeries that impacted my voice, my strength, and even my identity, I came face to face with the truth that healing is a journey. There's a sacred slowness in how God restores.

The "recovery room" is not a place of punishment—it's a place of preparation.

It's where God re-centers your focus, reminds you who you are, and refines your dependence on Him.

I learned that healing doesn't always look like immediate deliverance. Sometimes it looks like a renewed perspective.

Sometimes it looks like learning how to breathe again in broken places.

Story/Testimony

In 2016, I was ordained. It was a spiritual high point—a confirmation of calling, purpose, and identity. Yet, shortly after that mountaintop moment, the fire came.

In 2018, I underwent cervical spine surgery—a painful, complex procedure that left me more than physically wounded. I was mentally and spiritually exhausted. My body needed rest, but so did my soul. And it was in that quiet place of recovery that God met me.

The healing process was grueling. I had to wear a halo support helmet to stabilize my cervical spine—an experience that was nearly unbearable. But that was only the tip of the iceberg.

During the procedure, the surgeon made an incision at the front of my neck. To access my cervical spine, he had to carefully move soft tissues—including my vocal cords. While the surgery was successful structurally, it came with unexpected consequences: my vocal cord was damaged, and I lost the ability to speak clearly.

I could still talk, but only with a severely raspy voice. Worse yet, I could no longer swallow properly. Whether drinking or eating, I would often choke, because the damage had left a gaping space between my vocal cords. I had lost control over the muscles required to swallow—a terrifying and demoralizing reality.

I was frustrated, distraught, angry, and confused. I didn't expect to come out of surgery broken—I expected to come out healed.

Months passed as my doctor searched for a specialist who could help. Eventually, I was referred to an ENT doctor who specialized as a laryngologist. This referral became a turning point.

I underwent multiple tests—X-rays, MRIs—and endured uncomfortable procedures. But what broke me emotionally was the nerve test. Imagine a doctor telling you they need to test the electrical current in your vocal cords to see if there's paralysis. Then imagine them using a long, thin needle to pierce the muscle in your vocal cord while you're fully awake.

It was painful beyond description. I still quiver just thinking about it. I can remember looking over and seeing the expression on my wife's face—her eyes wide, her body tense. She didn't say a word, but her face said it all: "This looks unbearable."

As the needle pierced my throat, I began to pray silently: "God, give me the strength not to move—especially with this needle inside my neck. Help me endure this. Numb me so I won't break." And God did just that. I made it through the test.

But the news was crushing: my right vocal cord was paralyzed.

Despite the grim diagnosis, there was a glimmer of hope. A surgical option—a vocal cord implant—offered a chance to restore my voice.

Later, I underwent the implant procedure. As someone called to speak and teach, losing my voice had felt like losing my purpose. But when God restored my voice, I understood something even greater: He hadn't just healed my throat—He had refined my message.

What I thought was the end of my usefulness turned out to be a divine transition. In the silence, God spoke. In the stillness, God healed.

Influence

When you walk through healing and restoration, your influence deepens. People don't listen because you're perfect—they listen because you've endured. Your scars become signs of hope to others still lying on the operating table or waiting in their own recovery room. Each time I share how God healed my voice and renewed my strength, someone else dares to believe that healing is possible for them too.

Your healing carries weight—not just for your own life, but for those watching how you navigate the journey. The way you walk through adversity can become someone else's roadmap to faith.

During my recovery, I found hope in the example of Joseph, particularly in Genesis 39:10–23. Even when Joseph was falsely accused, imprisoned, and forgotten by man, he was never forgotten by God. His story reminded me that purpose can still thrive even when life feels like a prison.

Likewise, in my darkest moments—when it felt like my voice, my strength, and even my purpose were fading—I was held up by the unwavering love of my wife, my mother, and my family. Their encouragement anchored me. They refused to let me give up. They reminded me that the unexpected does not erase God's plan. His purpose still stands—even when the process is painful.

Their faith in me helped restore my faith in God's bigger picture. I came to realize that my story, with all its detours and disappointments, was still divinely designed.

Scripture Insight

Joel 2:25 — *"I will restore to you the years that the swarming locust has eaten…" God doesn't just heal—He redeems time and renews what seemed lost forever.*

Psalm 147:3 — *"He heals the brokenhearted and binds up their wounds." Healing is both internal and external. God works through every layer of our being.*

Psalm 30:11–12 — *Your mourning isn't wasted. He turns weeping into dancing, and your silence into praise.*

Biblical Pattern of Breaking Points

Healing is a sacred process, not a rushed event. The "recovery room" of life is where God applies His gentle grace, mends wounds, and restores identity. What feels like a pause is actually a preparation.

So many in Scripture found restoration on the other side of their breaking:

- **Naaman** had to dip in muddy water before his leprosy was cleansed (2 Kings 5).
- **The woman with the issue of blood** found healing only after years of pain—and pressing through the crowd (Mark 5).
- **Job**, after unimaginable suffering, was restored double (Job 42:10).

Each breaking was followed by a slow but undeniable rebuilding. God works not just through *miracles*, but through *processes*.

Reflection Questions

1. What are some ways God sustained you during your "recovery room" season?
2. When have you felt tempted to rush healing, and what did God teach you instead?
3. What part of your recovery has become a ministry to someone else?
4. How do you see the hand of God in your healing journey now that you're further along?

Application

- Journal each week about small signs of restoration—emotional peace, physical energy, relational healing.

- Reflect: Am I trusting God's pace, or demanding immediate results?
- Create a testimony timeline: mark key moments of healing or turning points to remember and share.
- List three ways God has restored something in your life (peace, relationships, voice, etc.).

Prayer & Encouragement

Prayer:

Jesus, thank You for Your grace that carries us when we feel too weak to carry ourselves. In every weary step and every sleepless night, You have been present. Remind us that we are not alone in the waiting, not forgotten in the silence, and not abandoned in the slow process of healing.

Jehovah Rapha, heal our bodies, our minds, and our souls. Restore what was broken in ways only You can. Thank You for not rushing our recovery but for walking with us through every phase of it. Where we have felt empty, fill us again. Where we have been silenced, speak life over us. Where we have been still, stir purpose within us.

We choose to trust Your pace. We lean into Your presence. And we believe that even in this recovery room, You are doing a holy work in us. Amen.

Encouragement

You are not behind. You are not failing. Healing is not a straight line—and you're not late to your own recovery. God sees every tear you've cried in silence, every ache you've endured without applause, and every small step forward that no one else noticed.

The recovery room is not punishment—it's preparation. It's where God strengthens what was once weak, restores what was once broken, and redefines what you thought was lost. Your scars don't disqualify you—they qualify you to speak healing into others. What you've endured has made your testimony weighty, powerful, and personal.

If you're still in the recovery process, don't rush it. Stay where grace is doing the slow, unseen work. And remember this: *What God restores, He strengthens. What He strengthens, He uses. And what He uses—He multiplies for His glory.* Hold on. Healing is happening—even here.

Quote to Remember:
"Healing isn't fast—but grace is faithful in every slow step."

Journal / Notes:
(Write your reflections here)

Chapter 6

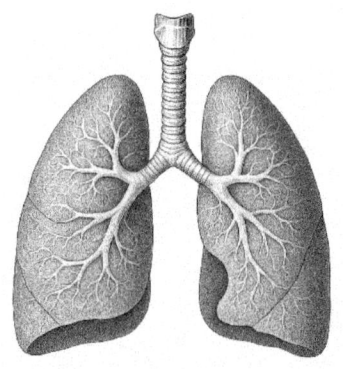

Breathless But Believing

Psalm 118:17
"I will not die but live, and will proclaim what the Lord has done."

Romans 8:2
"And we know that in all things God works for the good of those who love him."

Introduction

Near-death moments have a way of clarifying what matters. During COVID pneumonia, I was gasping for air, but my spirit clung to faith. When breath was short, belief carried me. Perspective changes everything. Even the most painful seasons can reveal God's glory when we choose to see through eyes of faith. This chapter invites you to reframe your story—not to erase the pain, but to find God's purpose in it.

Key Takeaway:

"Even when life leaves you breathless, faith gives you strength to live."

Expanded Reflection

Breath is something we take for granted—until it's no longer easy. In those agonizing moments when every inhale feels like a battle, we are reminded of how fragile life truly is. But faith thrives in the fragile. The very moments that leave us weak are often the ones that make room for divine strength.

To be breathless and yet believing is to say, "God, even when I don't understand, I trust You." It is a surrender that doesn't deny fear but overcomes it. It's in the hospital bed, in the isolation, in the sleepless nights, where God whispers, "You're still here—for a reason."

Sometimes, God allows the breath to be shortened so our dependence on Him can deepen. In this way, suffering becomes sacred. It becomes the soil where endurance, gratitude, and trust are grown.

Story/Testimony

One of the most terrifying experiences I've ever faced occurred during the height of the COVID-19 pandemic. This was a time when breathing complications became the leading cause of death around the world. People who entered emergency rooms with hope of recovery often never made it back home. Many were placed on ventilators after their oxygen levels plummeted to dangerously low levels—and tragically, a large number of those patients never came off. What made it even more heartbreaking was the isolation: people died alone, separated from loved ones, with only the quiet presence of medical staff nearby. That reality alone can shake your faith and bring fear to the forefront of your mind.

And then—I became one of them.

I was diagnosed with severe COVID pneumonia. My condition deteriorated so quickly that if my wife hadn't taken me to the hospital when she did, I truly don't know if I would've survived. At home, I had a violent, unrelenting cough and was so weak I couldn't walk the ten steps from my bed to the bathroom without nearly passing out. My oxygen levels dropped into the low 80s—far below what's safe. We both went to get checked, but I couldn't even make it into the building. I had to be wheeled in and placed on oxygen just to stabilize me.

Tests confirmed what we feared: over 65% of my lung capacity was consumed by pneumonia.

I couldn't breathe. I couldn't move. I couldn't get out of bed without supplemental oxygen.

I was taken to a specialized, isolated emergency room. No family. No visitors. Just me, some machines, and the quiet presence of nurses and doctors. I lay there—scared, disoriented, and emotionally drained—knowing this was exactly the scenario many others had faced… right before they died.

For seven days, I battled alone. The silence was deafening. Every beep from the machines felt like a countdown. Every shallow breath whispered, *"Is this it?"* I thought of everything I hadn't done, words I hadn't said, prayers I hadn't finished.

Would I make it out? Or would I become another statistic?

But in that breathless moment, I heard God's promise deep in my spirit: **"You shall live and not die."** That whisper became a turning point. What began as a medical emergency turned into a spiritual encounter. God met me right in the middle of my isolation.

Though my wife and kids weren't allowed inside, they stood outside my hospital window—faithful, present, praying. My wife brought me my iPad and Bible. I couldn't sing or shout, but I could read. I could weep. I could trust. And so, I worshipped with every breath I had left.

When life feels like it's unraveling and despair seems closer than hope, it's hard to hold on. But sometimes, hope doesn't need to be held—*hope finds you.*

Even when I couldn't pray aloud…
Even when I couldn't walk across the room…
Even when my lungs couldn't carry a full breath…

God carried me.

Each inhale became an act of worship. Each blink, a declaration of purpose. I realized God didn't just spare me—He strengthened me. He turned my panic into praise and my shortness of breath into a testimony of His sustaining power.

As time passed, my oxygen levels slowly began to rise. I was eventually discharged from the hospital, sent home with supplemental oxygen and a renewed sense of purpose. For the next two months, every breath I took at home reminded me of God's mercy. Each step I regained, each night I rested without fear, became a silent praise for the God who brought me through. Though I was still physically weak, I was spiritually stronger than I had ever been. By the grace of God, my lungs healed, and my oxygen levels rose back to 100%. Healing came not just to my body—but to my faith, my mindset, and my calling.

Looking back, I see now that God wasn't just restoring my breath—He was restoring my voice to proclaim His faithfulness.

Influence

My story of survival became a testimony for others walking through sickness, fear, and uncertainty. Family, friends, and even strangers began telling me how encouraged they were to see me trust God through suffering. People who had given up on prayer said they started praying again because they saw what God did for me. Nurses told me I inspired them to care with more compassion. What I once saw as a personal crisis, God turned into a platform of healing for others.

Scripture Insight

Romans 8:28 reminds us: *"And we know that in all things God works for the good of those who love Him, who have been called according to His purpose."* This verse doesn't promise that everything will feel good, but that everything will be used for good in God's hands. It shifts the lens through which we see suffering.

2 Corinthians 1:9 declares: *"But this happened that we might not rely on ourselves but on God, who raises the dead."* Sometimes it takes a breaking point to recognize that our strength is not enough. But when God steps in, even death loses its grip.

Psalm 118:17 reminds us of our reason to live: *"I will not die but live, and will proclaim what the Lord has done."* This isn't just about survival—it's about purpose. Every spared breath is a chance to proclaim God's faithfulness.

Biblical Pattern of Breaking Points

> *When life strips us of control—of breath, of certainty—it's an opportunity to trust God like never before. Even when you feel like you're gasping, your faith can shout, "I will live!"*

Many in the Bible faced moments where breath and belief collided:

- **Elijah**, after calling fire from heaven, found himself in a cave asking God to take his life. God instead restored him and gave him purpose.
- **Paul**, repeatedly beaten, shipwrecked, and imprisoned, testified of God's strength in his weakness: *"When I am weak, then I am strong."* (2 Corinthians 12:10)
- **Job**, afflicted beyond comprehension, said, *"Though he slay me, yet will I hope in him."* (Job 13:15)

These stories echo the truth: faith doesn't eliminate suffering—but it transforms it. When we are at our lowest, God often shows us a higher view of His power and purpose.

Reflection Questions

1. Have you ever experienced a moment where your health or circumstances left you feeling breathless—physically, emotionally, or spiritually? What did that moment reveal about your faith?
2. How did God make His presence known to you in your weakest hour? Was it through Scripture, a person, a moment of clarity, or something else?
3. When fear or uncertainty overwhelmed you, what did you choose to believe about God's character?
4. What does "living on purpose" mean to you now that you've faced the possibility of not surviving?
5. What spiritual or emotional healing still needs to take place from that experience?
6. How can your story bring breath and belief to someone else who may feel like they are barely holding on?

Application

- Write your own declaration of faith beginning with: "Even when I feel breathless, I believe that..."
- Reflect on how this near-death experience clarified what really matters.
- Spend time praying and thanking God specifically for the breath in your lungs today.

Prayer & Encouragement

Prayer:

Father, when I couldn't breathe, You breathed over me. When I felt like giving up, You held me up. I thank You that I am still here—not by accident, but by assignment. Help me to see every breath as a gift and every moment as a chance to honor You. Heal the places in me that are still weary. Use my story to bring light to others in darkness. And remind me that even in my weakest hour, You are still God, and I am still Yours. In Jesus' name, Amen.

Encouragement

You didn't just survive—you were sustained. You are living proof that God's hand is stronger than any sickness, and His purpose is bigger than any diagnosis. Keep breathing. Keep believing. Your breath is a testimony.

Quote to Remember:
"Even when life takes your breath, faith gives you reason to keep breathing."

Journal / Notes:

(Write your reflections here)

Chapter 7

Still Standing

2 Corinthians 12:9
"My grace is sufficient for you, for My power is made perfect in weakness."

Isaiah 40:31
"But those who hope in the Lord will renew their strength. They will soar on wings like eagles; they will run and not grow weary; they will walk and not be faint."

Introduction

Life has tried to take you out—but you're still here. You're not just surviving; you're standing. That's God's grace.

Key Takeaway:

"Your survival is proof of God's sustaining power."

Expanded Reflection

To be *still standing* is more than survival—it's a testament to God's sustaining grace. Life throws punches: loss, sickness, disappointment, spiritual fatigue. Each one feels like it could be the final blow. But when the storm passes and you realize you're still here, you begin to see that God's grace wasn't just enough—it was abundant.

Standing does not mean unshaken or untouched. It means that even though you've been hit, you're still moving forward. God strengthens us in the stillness. Isaiah 40:31 reminds us that our hope renews us—not our hustle, not our strength, but our *hope*. The enemy expected you to quit. Life expected you to fold. But grace gave you grit. And that grit has kept you grounded in the truth that your life has purpose.

Story/Testimony

There were times when I felt too weak to continue—when the burdens were heavier than I could bear and the darkness felt like it would swallow me whole. There were days I laid in bed, too exhausted to move, fighting through pain in my body and confusion in my mind. The enemy whispered that I was done. That my best days were behind me. That everything I had poured into others was meaningless now because I couldn't even help myself.

But it was then—precisely in those lowest, most fragile moments—that God's grace met me. Not as a thunderous roar, but as a quiet whisper that said, *"You're not finished yet."*

I remember nights when I cried out to God, "Why this, Lord? Why so many battles back-to-back?" I had faced the crushing grief of losing loved ones, including the death of my father and most recently, my grandmother who raised me. I walked through chronic illness, disability, unemployment, and surgery after surgery. My body had been broken down by a degenerative spinal disease. I had endured a TIA, had a vocal cord implant, survived COVID pneumonia, and was still waking up each day to new pain. Each one of these trials could have been the moment I gave up. But God never let go.

In 2023, after earning my doctorate—a milestone that should have brought joy and new opportunities—I instead found myself unemployed and overlooked. I wondered why doors wouldn't open after I had worked so hard. I was physically tired, emotionally drained, and spiritually on the verge of collapse. Yet somehow, through all of that, I kept waking up. Kept pressing forward. Kept breathing.

Not because I was strong. But because grace was strong for me.

I've discovered that "still standing" doesn't mean I haven't been knocked down. It means every time I was—grace picked me up.

It means that when others saw the shell of who I used to be, God saw the blueprint of who He was still molding me to become.

It means that when the grief of losing my grandmother, the woman who raised me like a son, nearly broke my spirit in 2025, God carried me through the funeral, the sleepless nights, and the silent pain that followed.

It means that even when depression tried to settle in like a fog, God's light kept piercing through.

I may have scars. I may walk with a limp in my soul. But every mark on my life is a reminder that I've been through the fire—and lived to tell about it.

Still standing doesn't mean life has been fair—it means God has been faithful.

Still standing means I've buried loved ones, lost parts of myself I never thought I'd get back, sat in waiting rooms for hours, and listened to doctors tell me things I didn't want to hear—but somehow, I'm still here.

I've stood at gravesites and hospital beds.

I've stood in pulpits and prayer closets.

And through it all, God stood with me.

There is power in that testimony—not because I am remarkable, but because grace is. The kind of grace that meets you in your lowest valley, wipes your tears, and whispers, *"You're not done yet."*

If you're reading this and wondering how you're going to make it, let me remind you: if you're still standing, it's not by accident—it's by assignment.

You may feel like you've lost too much to keep going, but I promise you—God is preserving what's left for a purpose that still has power.

So stand, even if you're shaking. Stand, even if you have to do it in tears. Stand, because grace is holding you up when everything else falls apart.

And one day, you'll look back like I have—not with regret, but with reverence. Because what tried to break you didn't win. Grace did.

Influence

Your ability to endure has a ripple effect. You may not realize it, but people are watching how you respond to pressure. Your perseverance preaches louder than words. Someone else is learning how to stand because they saw you refuse to fall apart. You become a beacon of resilience—a testimony that pain does not have to have the final say.

Friends, family, and even strangers are impacted when they see scars that haven't turned you bitter. Your scars testify: "Yes, I've been through it. But God brought me out." Sometimes, your influence isn't about what you say—but how you *live* after the fall.

Scripture Insight

2 Corinthians 12:9 speaks to the heart of the chapter's message: *"My grace is sufficient for you, for My power is made perfect in weakness."* Paul wrote these words after pleading for God to remove a thorn—a personal struggle that remained. Instead of healing, God offered him something greater: sustaining grace. That grace didn't change Paul's circumstance, but it transformed his outlook. Weakness became the stage where God's power was best displayed.

Isaiah 40:31 reveals another layer: those who *hope* in the Lord are *renewed*. This isn't mere emotional strength—it's divine restoration. Standing doesn't mean soaring all the time. Sometimes standing means walking and not fainting. And even that is a miracle.

When we rely on His grace, we discover power and peace beyond our own abilities.

Romans 5:3–4 — "Suffering produces perseverance; perseverance, character; and character, hope."

Psalm 91:7 — "A thousand may fall at your side… but it will not come near you."

Biblical Pattern of Breaking Points

Scars are evidence of survival. You're not standing because life was easy—you're standing because God's grace carried you through what should have crushed you. Your survival is a silent sermon.

68

Throughout Scripture, we find men and women who were brought to the edge of giving up—yet they kept standing because God stood with them:

- **Moses** was overwhelmed by the burden of leading a complaining people through the wilderness. He cried out in exhaustion and despair (Numbers 11:14-15), but God gave him help and strength to continue. *Still standing.*
- **Jeremiah** was mocked, beaten, and thrown into a cistern for speaking God's truth. He wanted to quit (Jeremiah 20:9), but the fire of God's Word within him would not let him stay silent. *Still standing.*
- **Paul** was beaten, shipwrecked, imprisoned, and afflicted by a "thorn in the flesh." But he declared that in his weakness, Christ's power rested on him (2 Corinthians 12:9). *Still standing.*
- **Jesus** Himself, though crushed and pierced, stood in our place on the cross. And though He was buried, He rose— *still standing*, victorious over death.

The biblical pattern is this: **When God is your strength, no breaking point can destroy your purpose. You may bend, but you won't break.**

Every time life pushed them down, grace lifted them up. And the same is true for you.

Reflection Questions

1. What moments in your life nearly knocked you down for good, and what helped you stand back up?

2. In what areas do you still feel weak, and how can you invite God's grace to be your strength there?
3. How has standing through trials changed your view of God's power and presence?
4. What role has hope played in your ability to keep going despite life's setbacks?
5. Are there scars in your life—emotional, spiritual, or physical—that serve as evidence of survival? How might they become part of your testimony?
6. How can your resilience encourage or uplift someone else who feels like giving up?
7. What does "still standing" mean for you today—spiritually, emotionally, or physically?

Application

- Practice daily surrender, acknowledging your need for God's help.
- Meditate on scriptures about grace and strength.
- Reach out for support when you need it; grace often works through others.
- Write a "survivor statement" starting with: "I'm still standing because…"

Prayer & Encouragement
Prayer:

Lord, thank You for holding us together when we felt like falling apart. Thank You for being our strength when we had none left. We've walked through fire, but we're not consumed. We've cried in the dark, but You were there. We don't always understand why we had to endure so much—but we believe that You are using it all for good. Give us the courage to keep standing, to keep trusting, and to keep moving forward in faith. Let our life be proof of Your power. In Jesus' name, Amen.

Encouragement

You didn't survive by accident. You didn't keep standing because you had it all together. You're here because grace picked you up, dusted you off, and whispered, "Keep going." Your story isn't over. It's just becoming more powerful. God doesn't just restore what was lost—He strengthens what was weak. So, take another breath. Plant your feet. And remember—you are *still standing.*

Quote to Remember:
"Your scars don't mean you lost the fight—they prove you made it through."

Journal / Notes:

(Write your reflections here)

Chapter 8

Telling Your Story

Revelation 12:11
*"They triumphed over him by the blood of the Lamb and by
the word of their testimony."*

2 Corinthians 1:4
*"He comforts us in all our troubles, so that we can comfort
those in any trouble."*

Introduction

Y our story has power. Testimony isn't just a retelling—it's a weapon. When you speak what God has done, darkness loses its grip. This chapter equips you to use your testimony boldly, as a form of ministry and victory. Healing is a journey, and it often comes with the call to step out of hiding and share our stories to encourage others.

Healing is not the end of the story—it's the beginning of a new assignment. I've come to realize that being healed doesn't mean hiding your past. It means boldly testifying of God's goodness, even if the healing is still happening.

Key Takeaway:

"Our stories are powerful weapons in God's kingdom."

Expanded Reflection

There's healing in honesty. For years, I misunderstood testimony as something reserved for a platform or pulpit. But I've come to see that sharing your story is not about spotlight—it's about surrender. When you testify, you're not glorifying the trial—you're magnifying the One who brought you through it.

Testimony isn't reserved for those with polished platforms—it's for the honest and the healing. Many people walk around in silence, believing their story is too messy, too painful, or too unfinished to be used.

But God uses broken stories to bring breakthrough. Your transparency is a bridge for someone else's healing.

Story/Testimony

Our stories of struggle and redemption have the power to encourage others who are walking similar paths. Sharing your testimony is not just recounting events—it's revealing transformation. It's declaring how God showed up in the middle of your mess and turned it into ministry. Every time I share what God has done, I'm reminded that the miracle wasn't just survival—it was becoming a vessel of healing for others.

There was a time I hesitated to share all of it. The pain. The surgeries. The grief. The quiet tears I cried after speaking engagements because my body ached from invisible battles no one saw. I feared people might see my weakness instead of God's strength. But God showed me that *transparency births transformation*—not just in us, but in those listening.

I remember standing at a pulpit one Sunday, my voice still fragile from surgery, my body weary from a week of flare-ups and restless nights. I didn't feel like a preacher—I felt like a patient. Yet when I spoke, something shifted in the room. People came forward, not because I had given the most eloquent message, but because I had given them my truth. And in my truth, they heard hope. They saw that faith doesn't deny the fire—it survives it.

One woman approached me afterward in tears. She said, "I almost didn't come today. I've been battling depression in silence, thinking no one could relate. But when you spoke, I felt like God was talking directly to me." That moment solidified what I now believe with all my heart: *testimony is therapy for the soul*—both for the one speaking and the one listening.

There's something powerful about saying, "I've been there. I know what it feels like. But God didn't leave me there." Your story might be the survival manual someone else needs. It might be the reason someone decides not to give up.

And so now, I share—not to showcase strength, but to showcase grace. My testimony is not about how strong I was, but about how faithful God is. He turned my breaking point into a breakthrough. He took what tried to destroy me and used it to develop me.

If I had never been broken, I'd never know the beauty of being rebuilt by grace. If I had never struggled, I might have never seen the strength God placed inside of me. If I had never told my story, I would've missed the opportunity to help someone else find theirs.

Influence

Your story carries influence not because you're perfect, but because God is faithful. Someone needs to hear that healing is possible. Someone is searching for hope—and your scars, your survival, your surrender can be the very bridge that leads them back to God.

Think of the woman at the well. She came to the well burdened by shame, but she left as a bold evangelist. Jesus didn't just change her life—He commissioned her to tell others. She had no title, no platform, just a story—and it was enough to change her whole community. Your influence grows not when you pretend to be perfect, but when you're honest about the One who is.

Your influence begins when you open your mouth and declare, "Look what the Lord has done."

Scripture Insight

Revelation 12:11 boldly declares: *"They triumphed over him by the blood of the Lamb and by the word of their testimony."* This isn't just poetic—it's prophetic. The enemy is silenced every time you speak what God has done.

2 Corinthians 1:4 says God *"comforts us in all our troubles so that we can comfort those in any trouble."* Your comfort isn't meant to be kept to yourself. Your testimony is transferable comfort. It's ministry in motion.

Psalm 107:2 commands, *"Let the redeemed of the Lord tell their story."* God doesn't just save us to sit in silence—He commissions us to speak.

Our testimony is a ministry of hope, healing, and transformation.

Ultimately, our trials are never just for ourselves. They're stories God entrusts to us to share, stories of hope, resilience, and redemption that have the power to change lives. Reflecting on my journey—from my father's death, through health struggles, and recent family losses—I now see clearly how each trial has become part of a greater story of freedom for others. In this concluding chapter, you're encouraged to boldly share your story, confident that your testimony can set others free.

Biblical Pattern of Breaking Points

In Scripture, some of the most impactful testimonies emerged from pain:

- **Joseph** was betrayed, enslaved, and imprisoned—but his story preserved a nation (Genesis 50:20).
- **The demoniac in Mark 5** wanted to follow Jesus, but Christ told him, *"Go home... tell them how much the Lord has done for you."* He became the first missionary in his region.
- **Paul**, once a persecutor of Christians, boldly testified of God's grace and wrote letters that still minister today.
- These stories weren't polished or painless—but they were powerful. Every breaking point became a broadcast point for God's glory.

Reflection Questions

1. What part of your story brings fear or hesitation when you think about sharing it? Why?
2. What platforms or opportunities has God given you to share it?
3. Who might benefit from hearing what you've been through?
4. What fears or hesitations do you have about sharing your story?

Application

- Start by sharing your story with trusted friends or small groups.
- Write your testimony to clarify and organize your thoughts.
- Pray for boldness and sensitivity as you share with others.

Prayer & Encouragement

Prayer:

Lord, thank You for giving meaning to our story. Even in the painful parts, You were present. Even in the broken moments, You were building something beautiful. Help us never to be ashamed of what You've brought us through. Give us boldness to share, humility to serve, and discernment to know when and how to speak. Let our words breathe life, ignite hope, and point others to Your redeeming love.

When we feel afraid or unworthy, remind us that our testimony is not about us—it's about You. Use our journey to unlock healing in others. Let every scar tell of Your faithfulness. Let every chapter reveal Your mercy. And may our voice never be silent when it comes to declaring the greatness of our God. In Jesus' name, Amen.

Encouragement

You may not feel like a preacher or a prophet—but you are a messenger. Your life is a living letter, written by grace, sealed by mercy, and delivered through every step you've taken. Someone is waiting on the other side of your obedience to speak.

You don't have to wait until the pain is gone or the story is wrapped with a pretty bow. Speak from where you are. Testimony isn't about having it all figured out—it's about pointing to the One who's walked with you through it all. You don't have to be eloquent. You just have to be honest.

Every time you share your story, heaven rejoices and hell trembles. You are *still here* for a reason—because your story still has purpose. So, tell it. Tell it with boldness. Tell it with tears. Tell it with joy. Just tell it.

Your voice matters.
Your scars preach.
Your story heals.
And someone needs to hear it—today.

Quote to Remember:
"Your testimony isn't just a story—it's a weapon against the darkness."

Journal / Notes:
(Write your reflections here)

Chapter 9

Purpose in Pain

Romans 8:18
"I consider that our present sufferings are not worth comparing with the glory that will be revealed in us."

James 1:2-4
"Consider it pure joy, my brothers and sisters, whenever you face trials of many kinds, because you know that the testing of your faith produces perseverance."

Introduction

P ain is never welcomed, yet it often becomes the place where purpose is born. In the darkest, most uncertain moments of life, God is doing a hidden work. This chapter reminds you that your suffering is not in vain—God is shaping something eternal through your temporary trial.

Key Takeaway:

"Our healing becomes a platform to minister to others. Changing how we see our pain unlocks God's purpose in it. Our freedom becomes a pathway for others to find theirs."

What you thought was just pain may be the very soil where your purpose starts to grow.

Expanded Reflection

Pain rarely announces its purpose up front. It intrudes— sudden, uninvited, and often undesired. But what if pain is the very soil where purpose takes root?

We don't usually associate pain with purpose. Pain feels like interruption, not intention. But if you've walked with God long enough, you start to notice—He often writes His most powerful chapters in the language of suffering.

Pain strips away illusions. It quiets the noise. It exposes what we rely on—and Who we truly trust. But beyond the discomfort, there is a deeper invitation: to find meaning in the mess. To allow God to redeem what felt like ruin.

It's in the valley that we find vision. It's in brokenness that God reveals the pieces of a divine blueprint we never saw coming.

Through the trials of grief, sickness, and loss, I began to understand that pain is not just something to survive, but something God can redeem. It taught me compassion. It made me sensitive to others' suffering. And it carved out in me a deeper dependence on the Holy Spirit.

There were days I thought the pain would define me. But God had other plans—He used it to *refine* me. When we give our wounds to God, He doesn't just bandage them—He builds from them.

Story/Testimony

Pain often feels pointless—until God reveals the purpose. What looked like a dead end was really a doorway to your destiny.

I used to ask, 'Why me?' But now I see how the pain prepared me to walk in purpose. Every trial taught me something God would later use.

I used to believe purpose only came from clarity and planning. That I had to get everything lined up—degrees, jobs, goals, ministry outlines. I thought I had it figured out. But pain changed all of that.

I never expected that chronic pain, disability, loss, and spiritual exhaustion would become part of my resume. I didn't want the role of the wounded one, the one who had to lean on others, who couldn't predict the next health scare or emotional hit. But it was in that very place—the place of loss, confusion, and surrender—that God began to show me what purpose really meant.

Purpose isn't found in perfection. It's found in perseverance.

Every painful experience—from surgeries to sickness, from loss to loneliness—forced me to lean into God in a deeper way. I had to stop chasing the platform and start embracing the process. I had to stop asking "Why me?" and start asking, "What are You doing through this?"

One night, during one of my lowest points physically and emotionally, I journaled a simple prayer: "God, if this pain has a purpose, please don't let me miss it." I didn't get an answer that night. But over time, He began to respond through people, through opportunities to share, and through unexpected ministry moments that came because of my pain—not in spite of it.

What I thought disqualified me—my struggle, my suffering—became the very thing that connected me to others. My vulnerability gave others permission to heal. My scars told a story that someone else needed to hear.

Chaos can feel overwhelming, threatening to steal our peace and cloud our vision of God's promises. As I navigated through grief, illness, financial uncertainty, and strained relationships, the chaos often felt louder than God's voice.

Yet, amid this turmoil, I discovered a peace deeper than circumstances, a peace rooted in divine assurance.

Influence

You may not realize it, but someone is watching how you walk through your pain. Your endurance is influencing more people than you know. Your silent battles have prepared you for visible ministry.

God doesn't waste anything—not even your tears. Every ache you've endured can now speak into someone else's life. Your survival is someone else's sign of hope. Your story can stir courage in those who feel stuck in defeat.

Don't underestimate the impact of your resilience—it may be the spark that ignites faith in someone else.

Scripture Insight

Romans 8:28 assures us that *"in all things God works for the good..."*—not in *some* things, but *all* things. Even the painful, even the confusing, even the silent seasons.

Genesis 50:20 reminds us that what was intended for harm, God *intended for good.* Your pain may have come through people or circumstances—but God can rewrite the ending.

2 Corinthians 4:17 calls our trials *"light and momentary"* compared to the *"eternal glory"* they are producing. That glory isn't just for heaven—it shows up now, when your story becomes someone's breakthrough.

Pain, if viewed solely as suffering, remains meaningless. Yet, pain surrendered to God becomes purposeful, powerful, and transformative. Reflecting on years of medical struggles and emotional wounds, I've learned pain is not wasted when placed in God's hands.

Biblical Pattern of Breaking Points

> *Pain is not the end of your story—it's the platform for your purpose. When surrendered to God, your wounds become weapons, your scars become sermons, and your suffering becomes seed for someone else's healing.*

Scripture is filled with stories of people whose greatest pain birthed their greatest purpose:

- **Joseph** was betrayed and imprisoned—but became a deliverer.
- **Esther** risked her life—but saved a nation.
- **Paul** was beaten, shipwrecked, and stoned—but wrote letters that still lead people to Jesus.
- **Jesus,** through the pain of the cross, brought eternal redemption.

Their pain was not in vain—and neither is yours.

Reflection Questions

1. How has God used your past pain to guide or shape your current purpose?
2. Who in your life may need the wisdom or comfort you've gained through suffering?
3. What pain are you still holding that God might want to repurpose?
4. How would your life change if you began viewing your wounds as tools in God's hand?

Application

Pain is not the end of your story—it's the path to your purpose. Ask God in prayer, "Who needs to hear my story right now?"

Prayer & Encouragement
Prayer:

Father, we give You the parts of us that still ache. We trust that nothing we've gone through is wasted in Your hands. Turn our pain into purpose, and our suffering into strength. Show us how to walk in freedom so that others may follow. Use our journey to break chains, bring healing, and glorify Your name. Remind us that what we thought was an ending was only a beginning with You. In Jesus' name, Amen.

Encouragement

If you've ever wondered, *"What was all this for?"*—you're not alone. Pain can feel senseless… until God reveals the seed it planted.

Your story may have chapters you never asked for—but those very pages may be what someone else needs to survive their own storm. Don't hide your pain—let it preach. Don't downplay your scars—they're signs of healing.

You're not just a survivor.
You're a vessel. You're a voice.
You're a bridge from pain to purpose.

Keep pressing forward—your purpose is unfolding.

Quote to Remember:
"The pain that tried to destroy you may be the platform God uses to deliver others."

Journal / Notes:

(Write your reflections here)

Chapter 10

From Test to Testimony

Psalm 145:4
"One generation commends your works to another; they tell of your mighty acts."

1 Corinthians 15:57
"But thanks be to God! He gives us the victory through our Lord Jesus Christ."

Graduation and losses (2022–2025) - Romans 8:37
"No, in all these things we are more than conquerors through him who loved us."

Ongoing strength to encourage others - 2 Timothy 4:7
"I have fought the good fight, I have finished the race, I have kept the faith"

Introduction

Every testimony begins with a test. What tried to break you becomes the story that builds others. God never wastes pain. He transforms it into purpose—and your scars into statements of victory.

A testimony doesn't end when the trial ends—it becomes a legacy. How you live today writes the story others will remember. This chapter is about claiming your voice and realizing the power of your personal story.

Key Takeaway:

"Your story may have begun in struggle, but it ends in glory— because it's God's story now."

Expanded Reflection

Your testimony doesn't stop when the storm passes—it only begins to shine. The test you survived becomes a story of strength, healing, and redemption. It becomes a tool in God's hand and a torch in someone else's darkness.

Many of us endure trials believing we'll someday "get through" them. But what if getting through it isn't the goal? What if the trial is meant to become a testimony that sets others free?

You didn't just survive—you were shaped. You didn't just make it out—you were made into something new. The test was never random. It was refining you for a greater assignment.

Your story is sacred. It matters. Not because it's perfect, but because it points to the One who is. When you speak about what God has done, chains fall—not just in your life, but in others who need to know breakthrough is possible.

Testimony isn't just about what happened to you. It's about what God revealed through it. It's about the transformation inside you, the worship that rose out of weeping, the faith that flourished through fire.

Living as a testimony means waking up each day determined to reflect God's faithfulness. It means using your scars to speak life, your survival to sow strength, and your setbacks to lift others higher. This is how legacies are born.

Story/Testimony

There was a time when I thought I had reached the end—after the losses, the health battles, and the personal grief. But God whispered, *"I'm not finished."* Each time I shared my journey, I realized the testimony wasn't just mine to keep—it was meant to give others courage.

I never imagined that the broken pieces of my life would one day help put someone else back together. I used to want a clean, easy story—no pain, no loss, no detours. But if I'm honest, that version of me wouldn't have had much depth to offer.

It wasn't until I faced surgery after surgery, buried family members I loved deeply, endured chronic illness, and walked through the fire of grief and disappointment that I realized: this is where the testimony forms.

I began to see God's fingerprints even in the trials. When I shared with someone that I had survived a near-death experience with COVID pneumonia, they wept. They were going through something similar and needed to hear that survival was possible.

When I spoke about losing my voice after neck surgery, someone else found the courage to believe that God could still use them despite their physical limitations.

And when I confessed to moments of wanting to quit ministry altogether, another leader said, "Thank you. I thought I was the only one."

That's the power of testimony. It unlocks doors for others to walk through. It brings light into places where people feel alone. It says, "You're not crazy. You're not weak. You're not alone. And you're not without hope."

My testimony didn't erase my pain—but it redeemed it.

Influence

Your influence isn't measured by platform or popularity—but by presence. When you show up with authenticity, honesty, and faith, people take notice. Testimonies open doors that theology alone cannot.

When you open your mouth about what God has done, you become a lifeline. You never know who's hanging by a thread, waiting to hear that someone made it through.

Someone somewhere is silently praying for a sign that it's not over. You could be that sign. You've endured. You've overcome. Now, your influence lies in your willingness to tell the story—over and over again.

Every "I made it through" becomes someone else's "If they can, maybe I can too."

Your testimony doesn't have to be wrapped up in a bow. It just has to be real. People relate more to your battles than to your blessings.

So don't hide the process. Share the struggle. And point to the Savior. Your scars are evidence that healing is possible. Your voice is a vessel for freedom.

Scripture Insight

We are called to live testimonies that inspire, teach, and encourage future generations. Your life story, especially the difficult chapters, can profoundly impact others, becoming a source of healing and freedom. Through every test I faced—loss, sickness, rejection—God revealed opportunities to encourage, inspire, and uplift others. This final chapter empowers you to see your story not just as a narrative of suffering but as a powerful testimony meant to liberate and transform lives around you.

Psalm 145:4 reminds us that *"One generation commends your works to another."* Your life is a sermon future generations will read. Don't hold back your stories of God's power—they're part of someone else's foundation.

1 Corinthians 15:57 declares, *"But thanks be to God! He gives us the victory through our Lord Jesus Christ."* You didn't survive on your own strength. Your victory is a gift—and a testimony.

Romans 8:37 says, *"In all these things we are more than conquerors."* You are not just a survivor—you're victorious through Christ.

2 Timothy 4:7 captures the heart of legacy: *"I have fought the good fight, I have finished the race, I have kept the faith."* Let this be your daily aim—not just to endure, but to finish well.

Biblical Pattern of Breaking Points

Throughout the Bible, God uses the stories of broken people to build unshakable faith:

- **Peter** denied Jesus but later preached the sermon that birthed the Church (Acts 2).
- **Job** lost everything but became a testimony of restored faith and double blessing.

- **Mary Magdalene**, once bound by demons, became the first to proclaim the risen Savior.
- **Paul** transformed from persecutor to preacher—his testimony shaped the New Testament.
- The **Samaritan woman's testimony** led her entire village to Jesus (John 4).
- The **man healed of demons** in Mark 5 wanted to follow Jesus, but Jesus told him to go home and *tell his story.*
- **Paul** repeatedly shared his conversion story—even when it put him in danger.

These stories reveal a truth: *your testimony isn't just your past— it's your ministry.*

Their pain had a purpose. Their faith wasn't just spoken—it was *lived.* And that legacy continues today through you.

Reflection Questions

1. What does "living your testimony" look like in your everyday life?
2. How have your past trials equipped you to speak life into others?
3. Who is God calling you to encourage with your story right now?
4. What parts of your test are still being turned into testimony?
5. How will you ensure your testimony lives beyond you?

Application

Your story has power—don't be afraid to share it. Reflect regularly on your growth and progress. Use your story to mentor or encourage others. Stay rooted in prayer and scripture as you move forward.

- Write your testimony in three parts: Before, During, After. What was life like before the trial?
- What happened during it? What changed afterward?
- Ask God for opportunities to share your story with someone in need.
- Record a short video or journal entry speaking your testimony out loud—you may be surprised by how powerful it sounds even to you.
- Encourage someone today by saying, "I've been where you are. Let me tell you what God did for me."

Prayer & Encouragement
Prayer:

Father, we thank You for every test that brought us closer to You. We thank You for turning our trials into testimonies. We may not have chosen the path we walked, but we are grateful You walked it with us. Use our story to bring light, healing, and faith to someone else. Help us not to be ashamed of our journey but to declare Your goodness with boldness.

For every scar that now speaks of survival, and every setback that prepared us for greater. We surrender our story to Your glory. Use every chapter—especially the painful ones—to encourage and set others free. Help us walk in boldness, speak with love, and shine with Your light. Make our lives a testimony that echoes beyond our years. In Jesus' name, Amen.

Encouragement

You've been through the fire and lived to tell the story. You are still—*still speaking, still standing, still believing.* That's testimony. Now it's time to share that story boldly. Let your testimony be someone else's survival guide. Don't hold back— your journey is the evidence that healing is possible, purpose still exists, and God always finishes what He starts.

You are living proof that God restores, redeems, and resurrects. You didn't just pass the test—you were transformed by it. And now, you carry a story that heaven celebrates and hell regrets.

The story you carry is sacred. Don't minimize it. Don't hide it. You survived for a reason, and that reason might be someone else's rescue. Your testimony is a weapon, a gift, and a light. Let it shine.

So don't be quiet now.
Tell your story.
Plant seeds with your survival.
Build bridges with your breakthrough.

And live so boldly that the next generation has no doubt what kind of God you serve. Your testimony is not just a chapter—it's the legacy.

Quote to Remember:
"You didn't just go through it—you grew through it. Now your testimony is your gift to the world."

Journal / Notes:
(Write your reflections here)

Final Words

Life's trials often tempt us to rush toward quick solutions or shortcuts to healing. Yet, the true power of transformation often lies in embracing the journey itself. In my own experiences—marked by health battles, career setbacks, and profound losses—I discovered that every moment, no matter how difficult, had significance in God's greater story. I invite you to slow down, trust the process, and find purpose and peace in each step of your journey.

Who in your life needs to hear your story right now, and how can you begin sharing it with them?

Invitation to Christ

If you've read this book and felt the tug of God on your heart, know that you're not alone. Jesus loves you and has already paid the price for your redemption. No matter what you've faced or where you've been, there is grace available to you right now.

Romans 10:9 says, "If you confess with your mouth that Jesus is Lord and believe in your heart that God raised him from the dead, you will be saved."

If you're ready to begin your relationship with Christ, pray this simple prayer:

"Lord Jesus, I admit I've sinned and I need You. I believe You died for my sins and rose again. I receive You as my Lord and Savior. Fill me with Your Spirit and lead me into the life You've prepared for me. In Jesus' name, Amen."

Welcome to the family of God!

What Is Your Testimony?

Use this space to reflect on your own journey. What trials has God brought you through? How has your pain shaped your purpose?

_____

_____

_____

_____

_____

_____

Scripture Index by Chapter

Chapter 1: The Breaking Point

- Psalm 34:18 — *"The Lord is close to the brokenhearted..."*
- 2 Corinthians 4:8-9
- Isaiah 43:2
- Romans 8:28

Chapter 2: When God Feels Silent

- Romans 8:26 — *"...the Spirit himself intercedes for us with groans..."*
- Matthew 6:6
- 1 Samuel 1:10-13
- Psalm 139:1-4

Chapter 3: When the Bottom Falls Out

- Psalm 40:2 — *"He lifted me out of the slimy pit..."*
- Isaiah 41:10
- Deuteronomy 31:6
- 2 Corinthians 12:9

Chapter 4: Faith in the Fire

- Daniel 3:24-25 — *"...I see four men walking in the fire..."*
- Isaiah 43:2
- 1 Peter 1:6-7
- James 1:2-4

Chapter 5: The Recovery Room

- Jeremiah 30:17 — *"I will restore your health..."*
- Psalm 147:3
- 2 Kings 20:5
- Isaiah 40:31

Chapter 6: Breathless but Believing

- Ezekiel 37:5 — *"I will cause breath to enter you..."*
- Job 33:4
- Psalm 23:4
- Acts 17:25

Chapter 7: Still Standing

- Ephesians 6:13 — *"...and after you have done everything, to stand."*
- Psalm 121:1-2
- 2 Corinthians 4:16-18
- Philippians 4:13

Chapter 8: Telling Your Story

- Romans 5:3-5 — *"...suffering produces perseverance..."*
- Genesis 50:20
- 2 Corinthians 1:3-4
- James 1:12

Chapter 9: Purpose in the Pain

- Revelation 12:11 — *"...by the blood of the Lamb and by the word of their testimony..."*
- Psalm 66:16
- John 9:25
- Mark 5:19

Chapter 10: From Test to Testimony

- 2 Timothy 2:2 — *"...entrust to faithful people who will be able to teach others..."*
- Psalm 145:4
- Deuteronomy 6:6-7
- Hebrews 12:1

Prayers & Promises by Chapter

Chapter 1: The Breaking Point
Prayer: Lord, when everything feels shattered, remind me that You are near. Help me see the breaking as the start of my breakthrough.

Promise: The Lord is close to the brokenhearted and saves those who are crushed in spirit. (Psalm 34:18)

Chapter 2: When God Feels Silent
Prayer: God, hear the cries I can't speak aloud. Strengthen my faith even when I feel unseen and unheard.

Promise: Before a word is on my tongue, You, Lord, know it completely. (Psalm 139:4)

Chapter 3: When the Bottom Falls Out
Prayer: Father, catch me when I fall. Let me land on Your grace and rise with purpose.

Promise: He lifted me out of the slimy pit, out of the mud and mire. (Psalm 40:2)

Chapter 4: Faith in the Fire
Prayer: God, I don't ask to escape the fire, only that You walk with me through it. Refine me through this trial.

Promise: When you walk through the fire, you will not be burned. (Isaiah 43:2)

Chapter 5: The Recovery Room
Prayer: Lord, use this waiting room to heal and prepare me. I trust Your timing and Your hands to restore.

Promise: I will restore you to health and heal your wounds, declares the Lord. (Jeremiah 30:17)

Chapter 6: Breathless but Believing

Prayer: Breathe on me, O God. When I feel weak, fill me with life, strength, and faith once more.

Promise: I will cause breath to enter you, and you will come to life. (Ezekiel 37:5)

Chapter 7: Still Standing
Prayer: Father, thank You for holding me up when I could not stand. Your grace is my strength.

Promise: After you have done everything, to stand. (Ephesians 6:13)

Chapter 8: Telling Your Story
Prayer: Jesus, show me the purpose in what I've endured. Don't let my pain be wasted—use it to help someone else.

Promise: What you meant for evil, God meant for good. (Genesis 50:20)

Chapter 9: Purpose in the Pain
Prayer: Lord, give me boldness to share what You've brought me through. Use my story for Your glory.

Promise: They triumphed... by the blood of the Lamb and by the word of their testimony. (Revelation 12:11)

Chapter 10: From Test to Testimony
Prayer: God, help me light the way for someone else. Let my journey serve as a lifeline of hope.

<u>Promise:</u> One generation shall commend Your works to another. (Psalm 145:4)

Acknowledgments

First and foremost, I want to express my deepest gratitude to God, my sustainer, healer, and ever-present help in times of trouble. Every trial shared in this book is a testament to His faithfulness and grace.

To **my amazing wife**—thank you for your love, your prayers, and your quiet strength. You have stood with me through every high and low, and I am better because of you.

To **my mother**, whose faith has been a light through dark valleys—thank you for believing in me and instilling in me the courage to rise.

To **my children**, you are my daily inspiration. Your love and laughter gave me strength on days I thought I had none left.

To **my brother** and **extended family**—thank you for standing by me, praying with me, and reminding me that I am never alone.

To **my friends**, both near and far, who offered support, encouragement, and shoulders to lean on—thank you for being present, even in my silence.

To my **church family**, your love, intercession, and fellowship have strengthened my soul more than words can express.

To **my pastor (Joseph L. Williams, II) and spiritual mentors**, your guidance, prayers, and prophetic insight have been instrumental in my healing and growth. You've helped shape my faith and fuel my calling.

And to **you**, the reader—thank you for choosing to walk through this journey with me. My prayer is that these pages don't just tell a story but ignite something in your spirit. May your life be forever impacted, and may your own testimony rise from the ashes of your trials.

About the Author

Dr. Derrick Washington is a passionate minister, retired disabled-military veteran, and servant-leader called to preach the life-changing truth of God's Word. With a **Master's degree in Theological Studies with an emphasis in Pastoral Ministry** and a **Doctorate in Information Systems and Technology**, he brings together both spiritual depth and practical wisdom to serve others with authenticity and purpose.

Derrick's journey to ministry wasn't conventional. Throughout his years in the United States Navy, he sensed the call of God—yet, like many, he ran. It wasn't until after his military retirement and relocation to Texas that he had a Damascus road encounter with Jesus that changed everything. In that divine moment, God made his calling clear, and Derrick surrendered fully to his purpose as a preacher and messenger of hope.

From Trials to Testimony was not written to seek sympathy—it was written to point people to the **Savior**. Through the pages of this book, Derrick shares how God's hands hold us even when everything around us feels like it's falling apart. His testimony is proof that **you matter**, your story has value, and God has a purpose for your life—even in your pain.

This book is a call to become **living testimonies**—walking, breathing evidence of God's grace and goodness. As Derrick often declares, "I have tasted and seen that the Lord is GOOOOOD!"

He lives in Crowley, Texas, with his wife and children, continuing to minister, write, and inspire others to walk boldly in their purpose.

Connect & Share Your Testimony

Your story has power. Don't keep it hidden. If this book has impacted you, I'd love to hear from you.

Email: inspiringfaithbydw@gmail.com

Website: www.inspiringfaithbydw.com

Share your testimony online using the hashtag #FromTrialsToTestimony

Together, we shine light for the journey of others.